The Horrors of War
From The Eyes of A Child

by John Dureke, Jr.

Published by:

JAHS PUBLISHING GROUP
4206 Gallatin Street
Hyattsville, Maryland 20781

Mailing Address:

P.O. Box 1164
Riverdale, Maryland 20738

Telephone: 301-864-2800
E-mail: info@jahspublishing.com
Order Online: www.jahspublishing.com

Printed and produced in the United States of America.

Library of Congress Control Number: 2002091870

ISBN 10: 0615498930   ISBN 13: 9780615498935

FIRST EDITION

Edited by Margaret Dureke, Wally Burns and Charlene Carter
Literary advice by Margaret Dureke
Typesetting by Wally Burns and Margaret Dureke
Art work by John Dureke
Cover designed by Wally Burns and John Dureke

SECOND EDITION published June 2011

ACKNOWLEDGEMENTS

Special thanks to the Ogwumike's, Achuko's,
Imehara's, Onochie's, and J. Okeke's
for accommodating the Dureke's during the war.

I salute the United Nations Peace Keeping Forces.

Thanks to Dr. Eugenia Oforndu
for her medical house-call program.

Thanks to JAHS Odiche Fitness and
JAHS Active Wear supporters and members!
Cheers to you all!

Thanks to Our Almighty Father!
My God is a Wonderful God!

INTRODUCTION

This book is about the horrific effects of war on a boy named P during the Biafran Civil War (also known as the Nigerian Civil War). The constant nightmares that P experienced show how war can precipitate multiple problems that are social, biological, educational, economical, psychological and traumatic for a child. All of these problems indicate that children who experience the horrors of war experience hard times at a very early stage and sometimes throughout life. Anyone who reads this book will have a better understanding of the impact of the horrors of war on children.

This book is based on a true story. The names of some of the characters in the book were changed to protect their identities.

TABLE OF CONTENTS

JAHS PUBLISHING GROUP
"Read and Be Inspired!"

FIRST STAGE OF THE WAR

In 1967, there was a little boy named P who lived in Enugu, in the Eastern part of Nigeria, with his parents and siblings. When P was ten years old, the country was caught up in civil war due to political and military strife. A major factor that caused the civil war was the 1966 military coup planned by dissident Nigerian Army officers from three major tribes - Igbo, Hausa and Yoruba. The military coup was successful in all areas of Nigeria except in the Igbo (Eastern part of the country). This was due to the fact that the coup plotters were arrested and detained before they could carry out their plans of assassinating top Igbo politicians. Mayhem, hostility and genocide were unleashed against the Igbos living in the Northern part of Nigeria. Igbos were hunted like wild animals, properties looted and destroyed, and thousands lost their lives during this stage of the crisis. One Nigeria was absolutely impossible at this point. The Igbos (Easterners) could not see any good reason to continue as part of Nigeria.

Tragically, the atrocities committed in the name of several military coups led to the death of many of our great leaders: Prime Minister Tafawa Balewa; Nigerian Military Head of State, Major-General Johnson Aguiyi–Ironsi; Northern Regional Premier,

Ahmadu Bello; and Military Governor of the Western Region, Lt-Col. Francis Fajuyi. The death of these great men ignited the flames of civil war, which were not extinguishable at this stage of the crisis. Given the massacre, mayhem, and destruction of properties of the Easterners, especially that of the Igbos, and since every negotiation failed, including the Aburi Peace Talks in Ghana, Lt-Col. Ojukwu, the Military Governor of Eastern Nigeria, with the advice and approval of the Consultative Assembly, declared the secession of the Igbos from Nigeria for their safety and security.

The Birth of Biafra

Eastern Nigeria became the Republic of Biafra on May 30, 1967. At this stage, there was no going back for the Easterners, although the Federal Republic of Nigeria said no to Eastern Nigeria becoming a separate nation. Therefore, within months, the Nigerian Army Troops, with the intent of reuniting Nigeria, attacked the town of Nsukka, which was located on the border between Nigeria and Biafra. Now that years of horrendous terror had been unleashed, some people degenerated to savagery and others used the bizarre times to put their cruel fantasies into practice. Wicked characters and dangerous people were placed in charge of some administrative positions where they played demigods.

Enugu under Attack

In the middle of one eventful night, P was awakened from a deep sleep by his mother. "P…P, wake up, get a few of your clothes and an extra pair of shoes," she said. P's mother told him that he would be leaving immediately because Enugu was being attacked by bombshells. P could hear the noise of the bombs:

Boom!! Boom!! Boom!!
Kwapau!! Kwapau!!!! Unudumm!!
Unudummmmm!!

P put a few clothes, his soccer ball and an extra pair of shoes in a plastic bag and got into a car with his mother. He looked out of the car window and saw a lot of fire on Milkin Hill. Noise from the bombshells was still being heard. Terrified, P held on to the plastic bag with his clothes and soccer ball, and as the car left the town of Enugu, the noise from the bombs subsided.

On the road, P saw a lot of cars, lorries and families leaving town. He saw soldiers in their camouflage uniforms on the road with guns and machetes. P was scared and confused at the sight of the soldiers. Most of the soldiers did not say anything to anyone. They just checked each car and told the drivers to proceed. Sometimes a driver was told to open the trunk of his car for inspection. Soldiers with painted faces and tree leaves covering their helmets were on the side of the road. When P passed them in the car, it seemed to him that the trees were moving. Some soldiers stood still as if they were trees; they were all beyond recognition. All of these unfamiliar sights frightened P and he asked his mother a lot of questions.

According to P, they were on the road for almost two and a half hours, mainly because of the road inspection by the soldiers. They passed truckloads of soldiers and armored tanks on the road heading towards Enugu, and the soldiers were singing:

> *"We are Biafrans fighting for our freedom*
> *By the grace of Jesus*
> *We shall conquer*
> *Someday, Someday."*

This terrified P even more, and he sat speechless in the back seat of the car wondering about the fate of his siblings and when they would join him. He thought about the speechless young soldiers that were barely holding on to their guns and rifles. A few of the young soldiers were his age, and P felt like getting out of the car and joining them, but he was too scared and still felt sleepy.

P at Ubomiri (Water bowl)

P suddenly asked the driver Joe when they were going to get to the village. Joe answered, "Soon – by 2 a.m." In a short while, P asked again, "Are we not there yet?" Joe answered, "In ten minutes." They finally drove into a big compound with a large mansion on the left side and other smaller houses on the right. Insects were making a lot of noise in the dark and P became even more terrified by this strange experience. To him, it was weird to hear all this noise at night without being able to see the creatures that were making the noise. There was no electricity and everything was dark. Although there was an electric generator at the compound, it was only used during certain times of the night and therefore, night lamps were used to welcome them.

P's Uncle Ike, a business tycoon, was a kind man. P's mother showed P one of the rooms where they would have to sleep. She remained calm and cheerful throughout the entire ordeal, which helped to reassure him. P's other siblings came the next day with their father, and their presence also helped to calm him down a little bit.

Living Adjustments and Horrific Encounters

P asked his mother when they would be going back to Enugu and she gently told him that they were now refugees and that this place was now home. P was shocked and worried about the new living arrangements and how he would adjust to the new life in the village.

When night came, P was told that he would have to sleep on the floor with his mat. He was scared because he had never slept on the floor before. That night P did not sleep very much. He kept tossing back and forth on his mat. P ran to his mother very early in the morning and told her that he had been unable to sleep. His mother responded that with time, he would get used to it. She told him to remember that they would soon go back to Enugu where he would be able to sleep in his own bed. She gave P a hug, but he showed no emotions because he was still very scared and confused by all that was happening.

One day P took his soccer ball to the football field to play with his new friends. He was surprised when he got to the soccer field because it was full of spikes made out of tree branches. There was no place to play soccer. P became sad and held on to his soccer ball as he headed home through a narrow bush path. On his way, he saw a long, skinny snake with a big head. The snake crossed the path very fast as if it were chasing some prey. This scared the hell out of P and he got goose bumps all over his body. He immediately ran home to avoid being eaten by the poisonous snakes meandering in the forest. Approaching the entrance to the house, he saw a scorpion, which ran and hid under a stone. In a panic, P removed the stone and killed the scorpion by hitting it on the head several times to make sure that it was dead.

At dinner time, P told his mother that he was not hungry, which surprised her because they were having his favorite food – yams and stew. P's mother asked him what was wrong and P recounted his encounter with the snake and scorpion. He also told her that he could no longer play soccer because of the war and the fact that the soccer fields were covered with spikes. P's mother said, "First of all, we are in the village where you will always see snakes, scorpions and other dangerous creatures. You need to learn how to avoid them. I will get Ofo to teach you some jungle survival skills, but know this for now – when a snake is not attacking you, run away, but when it is, get a strong stick and hit the head or use the stick to beat the neck so that you cut off its blood circulation. If a snake is about four feet long, go and get help! Whenever you see a scorpion, use a stone or stick to kill it. Over time you will get used to them being around."

"As for soccer, you can play in the small space under the trees with your friends since you do not want the warplanes to see you and fire rockets to kill you." P thanked his mother for the advice but was still scared.

At night P went to the toilet in the backyard. It was a hut with a small door and one window. When Ugo escorted P to the pit-toilet for the first time and pointed that it was in there, P asked with his eyes bulging out, "Where?" Ugo said, "Please, just go in there. The toilet is a covered pit. Just remove the wood cover, then after use, cover the pit." Ugo gave P a newspaper to use as toilet paper. When P opened the door, he saw the wood cover, which he removed. The pit was right there – a ten-foot hole in the ground. While P used the toilet, he kept on thinking that the snake would creep out of the hole, and the scorpion would be at the door waiting to sting him. Therefore, because he was anxious, P hurried and came right out, and Ugo escorted him back to the house.

P was a boy who had been born and raised in the city. Staying in the village environment was not a pleasant experience for him, especially with the forest all around. Moreover, dealing with the darkness at night without street lights was not easy. The noises of the night creatures seemed extremely loud because they were echoed by the forest. These noises caused P to have horrifying nightmares.

P kept thinking about returning to Enugu to go to school, and resuming the recreational activities in which he used to participate, like the Boy Scouts and playing soccer with his neighborhood friends: Charles, Samuel, Anthony, and Ike.

P kept on thinking and wondering what had happened to his old neighborhood friends: "Where are they now? Did they make it out of Enugu alive? When will I get to see them again? Will they grow up to be soldiers? Will I be in the same battalion with them?" These unanswered questions lingered in P's mind.

P scared and confused

SECOND STAGE OF THE WAR

In March, P's grandmother sent a letter through a family friend, saying that she would like for P to come and spend some time with her at Okigwe, another town. P was not excited because he had just made new friends like Ugo. He kept thinking about his school friends left behind in Enugu and how he did not even have time to say good-bye to Musa. P continually wondered if he would ever see Musa again because of the war. Now he would have to leave Ugo as well. P was beginning to realize that this is what happens in the life of a refugee.

Getting to Okigwe where P's grandmother resided became a problem because of the scarcity of gasoline in the area. The shortage was the result of some gasoline-producing refineries having been bombed by the Nigerian warplanes. However, it turned out that they had three gallons of gasoline in the trunk of the car, which was enough to get them to Okigwe.

P at Okigwe

On the morning of his departure, P hugged his mother who was holding his personal belongings in a small shopping bag. He then got into the car, which

Chike was driving, and waved good-bye to his mother as they drove away. The journey to the mountain town of Okigwe took them through rocky cliffs and trails. Chike drove in silence and P slept until they arrived at the home of P's grandmother, Nneka. When Chike woke P up, he was happy to see his grandmother, but was a bit surprised that they were on top of a hill. The Okigwe landscape was filled with hills and rocky mountains.

After P and Chike were welcomed, they took a bath. Then Nneka gave them soup and wheat, which they ate and thanked her for her kindness. P's grandmother called P to her and held both of his hands while she chanted:

> *"My great son! My great son!*
> *It is always good to see you;*
> *To see you is like when the moon comes out!*
> *You will be great like your father;*
> *You will always be protected by God!*
> *Thank you for coming!*
> *When I see you, I have hope;*
> *You will always come and go in peace!*
> *Welcome my son! Welcome!"*

After P and Chike had rested for about an hour, a group of village people came by and told Nneka that they were on their way to the nearby farm where a lot of chickens, hens and goats had been disappearing on a regular basis. The people of the village suspected that a big snake in the area was killing and eating the animals. Their plan was to go and find the snake and kill it. P got up and volunteered to go with them. Nneka instructed P to stay at the back and wait, and to learn how to hunt for snakes from the professionals. P was half scared, but thrilled as he joined the group that was made up of five men with hunting guns, knives, and clubs. Two young boys were carrying the bags for the men. P asked one of the boys named Okpara, "Can I help you?" Okpara responded, "No thank you, but you can hold a short club."

When the snake hunters got to the farm, everyone was told to spread out and look for snake prints on the ground. Ibe saw prints and called to the other four men who joined him. They followed the prints, which led them to a tree. On the tree, they saw a hole in one of the branches, which was filled with water. Ibe looked into the hole, examining and smelling the water. He then shook his head and stated that the snake was hiding in there. Ibe pointed the barrel of his gun into the tree hole and fired. He immediately put his hand into the hole and pulled out a big black python that was about six feet long. The snake tried to get away, but one of the elders stepped forward and cut off its head. The snake's head danced around for some time and the rest of its body was held to the ground with a stick. The hunters put the body in a big bag after the blood stopped gushing out. P asked Okpara, "What are they going to do with the body?" Okpara responded, "It will be skinned and used as leather after it has been dried in the sun." Observing this incident terrified P.

When P returned home and told his grandmother Nneka what had happened and how the snake had been killed, she told P that it would be a great honor when the day came that he would kill a big python by himself. P was speechless and could not believe his ears or even imagine doing such a thing. That night he had nightmares, cried, and shivered all night. Grandma gave him some coconut water to drink and rubbed dried snake oil all over his body to ease the pain. When morning came, P stayed home with Nneka all day.

One day Okpara came by and told Nneka that he would like P to go to the public square to watch the masquerades. Nneka consented and said that they should go and have fun and that it would be a good experience for P. She reminded P to run into the bush if a masquerade were chasing him, explaining that by doing so, they would stop chasing him. P and Okpara thanked Nneka and left.

On the way to the public square, the boys saw a group of kids and some adults who were throwing stones and clubs up into a palm tree. P asked what was happening, and someone out of the group pointed out that a cobra was on top of the palm tree.

When P looked up, he saw the black cobra with its flat head moving very fast from one tree to another as the group tried to stone it down. Suddenly, a hunter with a gun appeared and shot the cobra, and it fell to the ground. Okpara told P that they needed to move on and they ran to the public square to see the masquerades.

P saw a deadly cobra for the first time

At the public square, P and Okpara saw a crowd of people that were being chased by the masquerades with whips. The masquerades whipped anyone they caught. Everyone was in a happy mood, but P did not see this as fun since he was scared by the ugly appearance of the masquerades. However, P and Okpara joined the crowd anyway, and they were chased around all evening. P often ran into the bush for a break. At dusk, the masquerades left and the people went home.

When P got back home, he sang the song the masquerades were singing to Nneka his grandmother. The song went like this:

"I am coming! I am coming!
Are you ready? Are you ready?
It is only for those who can run.
If you cannot run – Stay home! Stay home!
And be a mama's boy or girl!
Uoo! Uoo! Uoo!"

Horrifying masquerades scared P
at the public square

Nneka was very happy that P was having fun. But that night, P told his grandmother that he was scared and afraid. Grandma gave him coconut water to drink as it was believed to have a soothing effect, and rubbed snake oil on his body to ease his muscle pain. Then she hugged P, told him some good bedtime stories, and said goodnight. Nonetheless, P could not sleep. He stayed awake all night without letting Nneka know. However, when daylight came, he slept until noon.

After keeping his grandmother company for seven months, the time came for P to return to his parents. Again Chike came and P said good-bye to Nneka and Okpara who were there to see him off. P cried and cried as he said good-bye. When he got into the car, P was extremely sad and exhausted from all he had experienced. He immediately fell asleep and slept throughout the entire journey home.

When P got to Ubomiri where his parents were residing, his siblings were glad to see him again. His parents thanked Chike for bringing him back, and P and Chike were served a welcoming meal of cornmeal and soup. P told his mother that he wanted rice, beans and stew, but his mother told him that they did not have any. There was a scarcity of food since the blockade by the Nigerian government prevented ships from coming to Biafra to make deliveries and the only food deliveries were by the night planes from the International Red Cross and church charities. P's mother said, "Please manage with what we have." P and Chike ate and thanked her. Later on, Chike returned to Okigwe.

P's Visit to the Refugee Camp

In the morning, P sneaked out and went to the refugee camp across the street, but when he got there, it was like a horror wonderland. He saw a lot of skinny kids and adults who where suffering from hunger and malnutrition. Some kids sat on the floor, some laid down, some were dying and some were already dead from hunger. P stood speechless and observing.

After seeing the suffering, starvation, frustration and hopelessness, he closed his eyes in anger and in tears, he walked away. In his mind, P sang the song he had heard from the Biafran soldiers during the fall of Enugu during the first stage of the war:

"We are Biafrans
Fighting for our freedom
By the name of Jesus
We shall conquer!"

P's Visit to Aba

One Friday, P's father John visited Owerri and told P that he would take him to Aba for a visit because he wanted P to stay with him for a while. P was not thrilled about the idea, but agreed to go because kids are not supposed to decide where they will go.

On their way to Aba, they were stopped at checkpoints by the soldiers, but once Mr. John showed his identification card and pass to the soldiers, they were allowed to continue on their journey.

P and his father ran into a big traffic delay on their way to Aba. They saw soldiers in camouflage uniforms with painted faces, who were carrying semi-automatic and automatic machine guns. When P asked one of the soldiers standing on the road what was happening, the six-foot tall soldier answered, "Civilians are just excited to see Lt-Col. Joe Achuzia who is on the road heading to the war front with some of his men." Lt-Col. Joe Achuzia, Major C. Nzeogwu, General Madiebo and Cpl. Nwafor were some of the names that evoked fear and hysteria in Biafra. On the Nigerian side were General Olusegun Obasanjo, General Murtala Mohammed and Lt-Col. Adekunle, "Black Scorpion"

Commander of the third Marine Commando, which had a special chant:

"Oooshebah, to keep Nigeria one
is a task that must be done.
Oooshebah!"

Hearing this made one squeak.

According to P, when you heard that chant along with military music early in the morning on Nigerian radio, it made you think about when all this would be over.

However, the Biafran S Brigade Commandos were one of the most feared elite units, and stories about their conquests were always told in Biafran. When P heard the name of Lt-Col. Joe Achuzia mentioned, his mind reflected on the dreadful stories he had heard about these soldiers, especially how they destroyed General Murtala Mohammed's battalion at Abagana.

P's mood changed as he sat back in the front and laid his head on the car seat. His eyes were wide open and his eyeballs protruded as if they would burst or fall from their sockets. His teeth were grinding as if he were chewing bubble gum. P got goosebumps and suddenly he fell asleep.

P and his father John arrived in Aba at night. The streets were deserted, and burning flames and smoke were noticeable in the sky. The minute P and his father passed a train station, a flashback about the horror train from the North was in P's mind. In his memory, the train was full of horror and sad stories. Most of the passengers on the horror train were missing body parts, due to the savagery committed by the Northerners, who had retaliated because some of their leaders were killed in the first Nigerian Army coup of 1966. They were angry because a number of Igbo army officers had participated in that coup. Consequently, some Northerners had decided to mutilate Igbos who resided in the North and put them on the train back to the East, the situation which P was now remembering. P had been an eyewitness to that train filled with horror at the Ogui Road Train Station in Enugu, on the day his Uncle Azuka returned from Northern Nigeria.

The Northern Army Officers' second retaliation coup of 1966 was yet another blow that melted the steel doors of reconciliation and made the horror train inevitable. Shaking off the flashbacks, P finally got himself together after letting his mind wander for a minute or so, but he still had a cold chill in his body. Reflecting on the air raids by Nigerian Air Force planes, the massacre of innocent civilians, and the destruction of properties in Aba, P remained speechless for several minutes and thought about what life was like before the civil war. He wished things could go back to the way they used to be.

P stayed in Aba for some time, but the daily bombing of the town and market, and the killing of innocent civilians by the Nigerian warplanes continued. Finally for P's safety, his father took him back to Owerri one day, where he would stay with his mother and other siblings. Again P was being moved, symbolic of his life as a refugee.

P horrified and in tears

One day at sunset, P saw the elders chasing away an ugly squirrel, which is a bad omen according to Igbo legend. Whenever you see an ugly squirrel, something bad will happen.

P's Family Relocates to Mberi

The following day, P's sister Uzo heard a special announcement on Biafran radio that there was heavy fighting near Owerri. Many Biafran troops were on the road – some in a lorry and some on foot. The troops were heavily armed with automatic and semi-automatic rifles, machine guns, and rocket launchers. Armored tanks were heading towards Owerri, and gunfire and bomb blasts were heard nearby.

That morning, Uncle Ike brought his lorry and other cars, and P's family and Uncle Ike's family loaded some of their personal belongings into the vehicles and left for the town of Mberi.

Along the way, there were many, many people on the road, and there was chaos and confusion everywhere. Most of the people were walking, carrying many of their personal belongings on their heads. Some were dragging their livestock; goats, cows and sheep. Mothers carried their kids on their backs; some mothers who had just had babies were walking very slowly because of their condition. The sight was awful.

Cars on the road were moving in slow motion as if they were heading to a funeral. Even the cars that ran out of gasoline or had engine problems were being physically pushed to the next town.

Many of the kids, young adults and elders on the road were suffering from malnutrition, and were struggling to walk to the next town. Some mothers looked extremely tired, but managed to put on a cheerful face just to show encouragement to their children. Some of the elders were too old to walk very far; they were walking in slow motion and often rested after only one mile of walking. There were teenage boys who were walking with their family's goat tied to a rope. Young ladies carried yams, plantains and other food for their families in baskets atop their heads. These scenes were not pleasant to P, and he was in tears from seeing all this suffering, painful resistance and determination. P wished that he was old enough to join the Biafran Army where he could make a difference. He said to himself, "I can't wait to grow up."

Biafran soldiers headed to the war front

P sat in front of the truck with Uncle Isi. When they got to the first hill near Mberi (Hilltown), Isi told P to look to the left side of the road. He said, "General Ojukwu, our head of state, is in that white car, with his army security soldiers." When P saw General Ojukwu, his fears disappeared because Ojukwu was the symbol of hope and victory for all Biafrans. P shouted, *"Power, Power,"* but the President did not hear him. He kept on looking at the crowd of people fleeing for their lives and safety. The heavily armed soldiers heard P and waved back to him. The last time P had seen General Emeka Ojukwu was in Enugu, when P had stood in front of his school shouting *"Power, Power!"* P had waved to General Ojukwu, and he had waved back. At that time, General Ojukwu had been on his way to address members of the consultative assembly (elders, leaders of thoughts, chiefs, and distinguished Biafrans) and members of the international press.

Refugees walked to next town

As P's truck drove by General Ojukwu's entourage, all his fears about the war disappeared, and P was very excited after seeing the General because of what he represented. When P and his family got to Chief Eze's[1] palace, which was like a big ship, P recalled his father's abandoned house in Enugu. Uncle Ike got out of the car, walked straight to Chief Eze, who was standing in front of his palace, and greeted him. Chief Eze welcomed everyone and showed them the apartment side of his palace where they would be staying. P made friends with Udo and Ama, the Chief's sons.

According to P, on the day of his family's arrival, most people paid special attention to the radio because General Gowon, the Nigerian Head of State, had gone on the radio and declared that the war would soon be over with the fall of the town of Owerri. But on Biafran radio, General Ojukwu told the gallant Biafran soldiers to fight on. Consequently, there was confusion and panic all over, and the people did not know what to believe. P heard the sound of gunfire all day and all night for two days. On the third morning, a special announcement on Biafran radio said that the Nigerian troops were landlocked and surrounded by the gallant Biafran soldiers in the town of Owerri.

---

[1] A man of the people and an industrialist.

The report said that the Nigerians could not escape and all would face their doom after they ran out of food and arms. The Nigerian soldiers were stranded in Owerri.

The next day, Ama came and called to P that they were going to the stream to fetch water. P told his mother and she said it was okay for P to go, but he should not swim because he did not know how. Ama assured P's mother that he would teach P how to swim. P and Ama left with their empty buckets. They walked down the hill and when they got to the river, they put their buckets down. Ama dived into the river, but P stayed and watched Ama swim for some time. Ama told P to get into the water, but to stay close to the shallow edge. He told P to pretend that he was riding a bicycle with his legs, and to relax his body and stretch out his hands. Also, he told P to pretend that he was clapping his hands. Suddenly P started floating. Then Ama told P to push his body forward, which he did. Ama instructed him, "Keep on practicing. You will make it. See you are now swimming."

Suddenly a snake appeared out of nowhere. Ama shouted to P, "Do not show any sign of fear. I will distract the snake." Ama started beating on the water, which frightened the snake, and it swam away as P swam to the bank of the river. Ama held on to the branch of a tree and swung to the bank of the river were P was standing and said, "Good move P! Whenever you come here early in the morning, beware of snakes." P was now trembling; Ama assured him that everything was okay and that he was safe. Ama lowered the empty buckets into the river and they filled up with water. P and Ama lifted their water buckets, placed them on their heads, and began walking home. Along the way home, Ama kept on singing:

"It is the brave
It is the brave
that survive a snake attack."

When P and Ama got home, they told their parents about their escape from the snake. The boys were reminded to always be on the lookout for water snakes at the river. P and Ama thanked them and left to relax for the rest of the day.

One morning while P sat on the steps in front of Chief Eze's palace, Ben came from the war front. Ben was Chief Eze's young son who was helping his uncle, Lt. Amobi, a Biafran army officer stationed at the war front. While Ben visited with his parents and prepared to return to the war front, P waited for him in the bush. Ben immediately walked over to where P was waiting. P asked Ben to take him to the war front, but at first, Ben was reluctant. However, P pleaded with him and said that it would only be for one hour. Finally, Ben agreed to take P along. It only took them ten minutes to get to the war front where Lt Amobi was stationed.

All living creatures except those humans who were soldiers had deserted the town. When they got to the house where Lt. Amobi was staying, he was not there. Ben gave P a camouflage army uniform to wear and P felt so good at this point. They set out towards the last line of defense, but they were told by the soldiers that they could not go any further because of the danger that a Nigerian Army sniper might shoot them. P had butterflies in his stomach, but did not show it. The boys left the war front through the bush trail, and P told the soldiers to convey his greetings to Lt Amobi. P made a victory gesture to the soldiers using his right fingers. When P and Ben got to the safe-talking zone, P thanked Ben for the experience of having been to the war front.

P terrified by the massacre of <u>innocent civilians</u>

THIRD STAGE OF THE WAR

One sunny day P sat in front of Chief Eze's palace. Suddenly there was a loud bang and a big flash of gunfire from the air that seemed like lighting and thunder. People ran for cover. P looked up and saw a Nigerian fighter plane firing rockets at the Chief's palace. After five minutes or so, the warplane flew away.

The Horrors of War

When the smoke cleared, Ifeyani and many others were dead from the gunshots. P's sister Ada, who had hidden behind a door, had been struck in the leg by a bullet. Windows and doors were shattered. Steel frames were bent and the cars outside were destroyed. The palms and other trees in front of the palace were ripped into pieces and their branches littered the entire palace yard. Following this mayhem and massacre of innocent civilians by the Nigerian Air Force fighter plane, people rushed to the palace to help the wounded and the dead. A head count was conducted; twenty people had died and about ten others had been wounded. Mothers were crying and all the kids were terrified – clinging and holding to their parents. P was mad and angry about this horrific tragedy; especially the gruesome death of Ifeanyi, who had a big hole in his stomach, with his intestines shredded into pieces and beyond recognition.

Suffering from the trauma of the fighter plane incident, P mourned the death of his friend Ifeyani and kept to himself for an entire week.

The tragedy brought by the fighter plane caused P to reflect on the early morning cries of mothers whose sons were killed at the war front. He also thought about an incident where a civilian was shot dead because he refused to be conscripted into the army. All these events were part of the horrors of the war that P witnessed.

In 1969, a Nigerian fighter plane attacked
Chief Eze's Palace; casualties were everywhere.
P narrowly escaped death on that day.

Christmas in Biafra

Christmas days in Biafra were the quietest of P's life. There were no celebrations, no new clothes, no new toys, no going to see the masquerades, no Christmas trees or decorations, and no visiting of friends and relatives on Christmas day. On some Christmas days, warplanes massacred and harassed the hell out of innocent civilians throughout the entire day.

P always remembered that before the civil war, the Christmas holiday was his favorite. He always got many gifts: toys, shoes, clothes, a custom cowboy outfit and toy gun, etc. However, during this war, none of that was possible. Daily survival was the important thing during that time. According to P, a bleak Christmas was the price of war. However, on Christmas night, P thought about Santa Claus. What happened to Santa Claus? Did the war chase him away? There was no more:

> *You better lookout! You better lookout!*
> *That Santa Claus is coming to Biafra.*

Now it was:

> *You better lookout and pray*
> *That the fighter warplane does not*
> *Kill you on Christmas Day.*

People said "Happy Christmas" and not "Merry Christmas" during that period because of the war.

P as a Refugee

P did not like being introduced as a refugee boy everywhere he went. In school, some of his peers laughed at him sometimes when the teacher called him a refugee boy by mistake. P got into fights with those who took the refugee joke too far. School could not be held daily because of the constant air raids by the Nigerian warplanes. Many days were spent in the bunkers. The continuous relocation, adjustments, and making new friends and leaving again after adjusting to a new town, made life as a refugee sad, embarrassing, and depressing.

The constant playing of marshal music on Biafran radio served as a constant reminder to P, that Biafra was still in a state of war. In addition, seeing soldiers suffering from shell shock always shook up P.

Another distressing occurrence that P always remembered was the early morning cry of mothers receiving the sad news that their sons had been killed at the war front. Their cries often broke the night's silence, keeping P awake until morning.

Seeing adults crying all the time was not a pleasant scene for P.

As a refugee boy, P had the opportunity one day to be at a town meeting of solidarity for the parents who had lost their sons at the war front. It was one of the most emotional meetings that P had ever observed. Most of the mothers broke down in tears as they grieved for their dead sons. Some fathers who had lost sons held their heads down to avoid eye contact and remained speechless. P said to himself, "I wish all this would be over some day."

Kids' Talk

When P and his friends got together they always talked about the war and shared their food. They talked about how they moved to the village from the town with their parents, and about how many uncles, cousins, and relatives they had in the army and their ranks. The kids mastered the ranks in the army from private to field marshal. When P and his friends talked about relatives that had died, some of them broke down in tears.

Chief held town meeting of solidarity
to console grieving parents

They also talked about the guns – automatic and semi-automatic rifles, and who made them, e.g. Mark Four, the Chinese assault rifle and S.M.Gs. Sometimes the kids sat around and sang war songs:

"Biafra will win the war,
With armored cars,
Shelling machines and heavy artillery
mortars."

P and his friends playacted soldiers with toy guns, standing and saluting each other in different ranks. When someone shouted air raid, they all laid on the floor or on the ground. And when the air raid was over they all got up. This drill helped in the real air raid situations. P and his friends would also choose the war front where they would like to serve. P chose Enugu, which was always on his mind. He missed Enugu a lot, and Enugu was always on his wish list to be liberated. When P and his friends talked about their favorite personality on the radio, they all mentioned General Ojukwu and Mr. Okoko Ndem (war reporter). P's favorite program was the Mberi Women's Program which served as a great psychological aid to P. One of their songs was:

"Greetings to all Biafran soldiers,
Greetings to all Biafrans,
All Biafran women can you hear us?
Please respond yeah, yeah.
If there is a conflict,

If there is a conflict,
I would run to my maternal home
to live and regroup."

After the song, they thanked all Biafrans and stated
that all should be vigilant and fearless.

FINAL STAGE OF THE WAR

After thirty months, General Philip Effiong, the second in command to our head of state, went on Biafran radio one day to declare: "All Biafran soldiers should drop their arms; the war is over; people should go back to their original homes and live a normal life; there is no more Biafra. General Ojukwu and other distinguished delegates have left for a peace negotiation." This was a special day with a lot of uncertainty in respect to the future. That same week General Gowon went on the radio and welcomed the Easterners back into Nigeria. He declared that there was no victor and no vanquished; rehabilitation and reconstruction would start immediately! P was thrilled. When he returned to Enugu, his father's house was still standing, but all the property inside had been looted. Some houses on P's street had been destroyed. Segu, a former tenant of P's father, wrote that he survived the war, but that he was now residing in London with his family. Finally, P could say that he had survived the war and lived to tell the story. But, over a million people died from the war. Some of P's friends were among the casualties of the war.

The Good News

P survived the war and went on to live a normal life, and became a big achiever like some of his friends.

Despite the horrors of war, we should not allow the tragedies of life to affect our plans for the future. We can always overcome the tragedies (ashes of doom) to become vital players in our community, state or country. With family and community support, it is very, very possible to succeed in life.

For the Sake of Our Children

The 30th of May of every year
remains a sacred day – just like 9-11-01!
My childhood life was put on hold
due to the war, but I lived on.
I saw the destruction of human civilization
through the horrors of war.

I saw the resistance, courage and
determination of my people, as they stood up
for what they believed.
I saw how they created and manufactured
things from limited resources;
How their genius emerged in the midst of the
blockade.

At last it came to an end.
But the horrors remain as part of history,
which needs to be told to prevent a recurrence.
We should always ask ourselves: Was it
worth it?
Hatred will never enhance human civilization –
but tolerance and peace will!

Tombs to be remembered

Advice to Present and Future Leaders

Advice to our tribal, regional, geographical, and spiritual leaders, decision-makers, policymakers and power elites: In order to enjoy democracy, we need to show restraint in our utterances and printed statements about government policymaking, especially during emergencies or crisis situations. Diplomacy through dialogue should be embraced at all times in order for democracy to reign. We should not allow our tribal, regional or geographical egos or sentiments to cloud our modest analyses, influence our policies, or lead to our unnecessary intervention.

We should remember that our utterances and printed words can make or destroy our legacy, depending on the reaction or perception of our followers, loyalists, or those governed. Situations or crises may get out of control, but our influence and diplomatic ability can win the day. If we allow situations to get out of control, they may explode in our face, maybe even after we have retired or left power. In such case, we would not be able to enjoy a peaceful retirement.

The fact that P had to hold back his thoughts and observations for years indicates that there may be many silent observers – silent observers who will speak their mind some day. To avoid the horrors of war, the actions of our leaders and the way they handle power under a democracy is very important. Remember that the children of Ogoni (Nigeria), Liberia, Sierra-Leone, Afghanistan, Israel and Palestine are observing and waiting to exhale. Thank God for the mass media because it is through them that the story is always told.

The new war on terrorism is a big warning and an eye opener to leaders that if you kill people while in power, you will not rest in peace and judicial justice awaits you. For those leaders who sow horror, judicial horror awaits them through the United Nations International Court of Law. So be advised!

Just as the birds fly and perch wherever they like, human freedom should be exercised freely without restrictions.

P's Advice

Sometimes disputes can lead to fights if not resolved initially. It could escalate to war like it did in this case. War creates death, bitterness, hunger, poverty, tears, despondency, frustration, sorrow, and bloodshed. Timely, peaceful intervention may prevent war; resolution is always possible.

Since human civilization should be preserved at all times, we should always try to prevent the horrors of war!

There is a saying that P always remembers, "No matter what happens, the sky will not fall." Living in a democratic society is always better and more psychologically gratifying. We should all try to preserve human civilization by living in peace.

Every day, millions of children experience the horrors of war. However, we can always prevent those horrors by respecting the rights of each other. To the millions of children all over the world experiencing the horrors of war – **Your cry is my cry! Be strong because it shall pass!**

Children experiencing the horrors of war are now the hero face of the world. The responsibility for keeping the world safe and democratic rests on our shoulders. Our forefathers passed along a peaceful world to us. We should endeavor to pass along a peaceful world to the next generation.

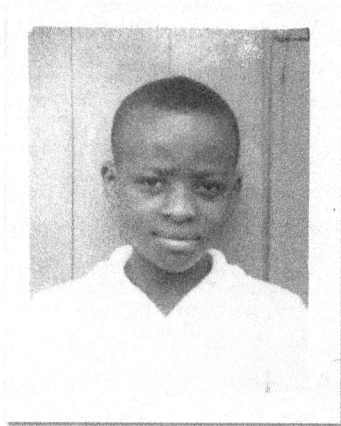

John Dureke in Biafra in 1968

ABOUT THE AUTHOR

Mr. John Dureke is the author of **"Z-The Goodluck Bird,"** a fascinating tale from the motherland that is full of folklore and practical advice. He is also the author of **"Acts & Portraits of Wisdom,"** an illustrated collection of African proverbs.

Mr. Dureke is the co-founder of the JAHS Publishing Group, JAHS Fitness and JAHS Active Wear based in Hyattsville, Maryland. He is married to Margaret Dureke, the author of **"How To Succeed Against All Odds"** and **"7 Drivers For Success."** They have three beautiful children. Mr. Dureke has an M.P.S. (Counseling) from the New York Institute of Technology; a B.A. in Political Science and a minor in Sociology and Anthropology from Hiram College, Ohio; and an A.A. in Political Sciences and a minor in Religion from John Cabot University in Rome, Italy.

Mr. Dureke is a recipient of the Helen D. Brown Award for Most Outstanding Student; the Youth and Child Care Worker Award from the DC Association of Youth and Child Care Workers; and an Outstanding Child Care Award from the Baptist Home for Children in Montgomery County Maryland. Mr. Dureke's success stories have been featured in many publications, including *The Washington Post*, *Afro-American*, and the *Prince George's Journal*, to mention but a few. John Dureke's work has been accepted in the movie industry in Hollywood.